WHO LOVES ME ALWAYS?

Second Grade Workbook

Marie Nachtsheim

Marie Fursman

Cecilia Crowley

Educational and Theological Advisors

Rev. Richard M. Hogan

Rev. John M. LeVoir

Mary Jo Smith

IMAGE OF GOD SERIES

IMAGE OF GOD, INC., BROOKLYN CENTER, MN
IGNATIUS PRESS SAN FRANCISCO

Nihil obstat: Mark B. Dosh
                 Censor Librorum

Imprimatur: ✠ John R. Roach, D.D.
               Archbishop of St. Paul and Minneapolis
               July 25, 1989

Cover design and illustrations: Barbara Harasyn

For additional information about
the Image of God program: 1-800-635-3827

Published 1991 by Ignatius Press, San Francisco
© 1989 Image of God, Inc.
All Rights Reserved
ISBN 0–89870–328–X
Printed in Hong Kong
Third Edition

TABLE OF CONTENTS

LETTER TO PARENTS

Dear Parents,

This year your child will be using the "Who Loves Me Always?" second grade program from the Image of God series. This series is centered on a new subjective emphasis found in the writings and teachings of Pope John Paul II. This subjective turn stresses the dignity of each individual as a person made in the image of God.

The second grade program has as its focus two key ideas: sacraments and commandments. These key ideas form the unifying element of the lessons. The material in each lesson revolves around fundamentals of our Faith stated in terms the children can understand and remember.

You, as parents, are the primary religious educators of your children. The "Who Loves Me Always?" program has many materials that are sent home to provide a basis for parent-child faith discussions. There are textbook pages for every lesson. Sometimes your child will bring home a completed activity to share. Sometimes, though, it will be up to you, as parents, to complete the activity with your child.

It is hoped that through this program you and your child will grow in faith together.

Unit 1:   GOD SHOWS US HIS
LOVE AND MERCY

Lesson 1: God Shares His Goodness

God made everything from His love. He made the angels. He made the whole world and everything in it. He made the sun and the sky. He made the land and water. He filled the land with beautiful plants and animals. The waters were filled with all kinds of fish. God made Adam. Adam was special because he was made in God's image. He could think and choose. Adam took care of God's world, but he was lonely. There was no one else like him, so God created Eve. Eve did not look exactly like Adam, but she too was made in God's image. Adam and Eve loved each other. They took care of God's gifts. Thank you, God, for your beautiful gifts.

God created the world. God made us special. We are made in His image. We can think and choose so we can love. God made everything else in the world for us to use and to take care of, except other people. We can help care for other people, but we may not use them.

Can you match the picture with the clue under each step? Write the number of the picture on the step above the matching clue.

1. Father
Trinity
Son   Holy Spirit

2.

3.

5.

6.

4.

He made everything. He always was and always will be.

This is alive, has no body. Has a mind and will. Can think and choose. Knows more about God. Is a person made in God's image.

This is alive, has a body, a mind and a will. Can think and choose. Is a human person made in God's image.

This is alive, its body moves and needs food. Has a brain, not a mind and will. It can't think and choose. It is not an image of God.

This is alive. It has a body, needs sun and water to grow. It is not an image of God.

This is not alive. It is not an image of God.

Can you see how people are different from the rest of God's creations?

Lesson 1: God Shares His Goodness

When God made the world and everything in it, He made us special. God made us in His own image! We have minds and wills so we can think and choose like God. We do not look like God, but we can act like God.

What do you think and wonder about?

Directions: Draw a picture of something you think or wonder about.

Lesson 1: God Shares His Goodness

A Reflection

You made me in Your image, God,
What does this really mean?
It means in everything I do
You should be seen.

You made me with a mind to think,
and a will so I can choose,
To know and love and serve You, Lord,
I'm made to act like You.

To be happy and do Your will on earth
You created me.
So that one day I can live with You
in heaven happily.

You gave me eyes to see Your world
and ears to hear Your voice.
Help me listen to You, Lord,
each time I make a choice.

For when I act the way I should
in good things I say and do,
I am who You made me, God,
I am an image of You.

God Shares His Goodness

Lesson 1: God Shares His Goodness

God gave us each a will. That means that we can make choices. What kind of choices do you make each day?

Directions: Draw a picture of something you made a choice about today.

When we make right choices and do and say good things, we act as Jesus taught us, and other people can see God in our actions. We are images of God.

VOCABULARY WORDS:

Image: A reflection.

Mind: What we think with.

Will: What we make choices with.

Person: Someone who has a mind and a will.

Human Person: Someone who is created in the image of God with a mind, a will, and a body.

Lesson 1: God Shares His Goodness

Directions: Circle the pictures where a person is using his or her talent(s) to make someone happy and is acting as an image of God.

Lesson 2: God Always Loves Us

Adam and Eve Disobey God

Adam and Eve lived in a beautiful place called the Garden of Eden. God gave Adam and Eve everything they needed to live forever with Him. God asked Adam and Eve not to eat the fruit from the tree of good and bad. If they did they could not live with Him forever. Adam and Eve loved and obeyed God and were very happy.

One day, the devil lied to Adam and Eve. Adam and Eve disobeyed God. This sin is called "original sin".

Adam and Eve lost God's life, grace. They could not always act the way they should. Adam and Eve left the Garden of Eden. They had to work very hard for their home and their food. They would suffer from the cold and get sick.

God still loved Adam and Eve very much. God gave them warm clothes to wear. God promised Adam and Eve that He would send a Savior Who would show all people who they were and how to act. The Savior would return God's love and show us how to return God's love.

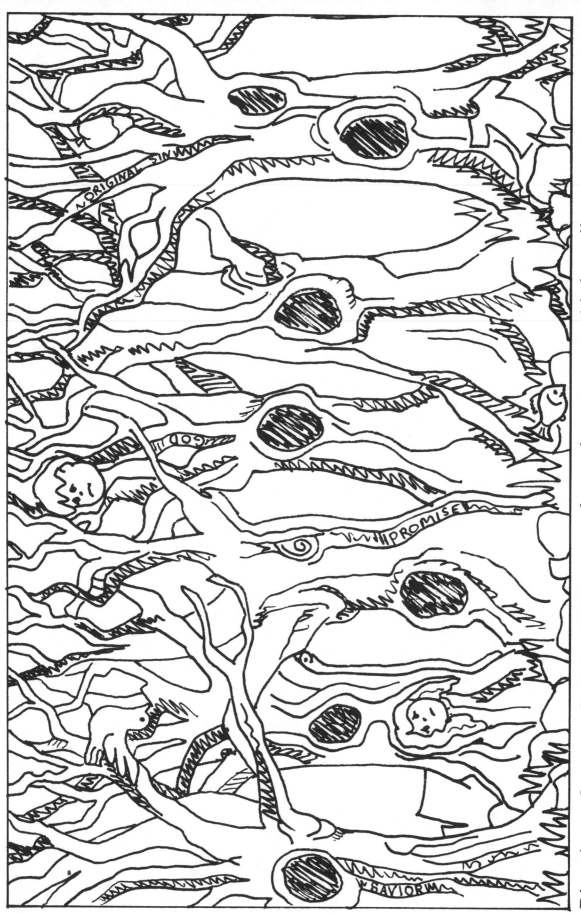

Directions: Can you find the hidden pictures?

Can you find these hidden words?

apple, snake, garments, bird, snail, Adam's and Eve's sad faces, fish

original sin, promise, Savior, God

Lesson 2 : God Always Loves Us

We are not robots. We have wills and are able to love.

Directions: Draw a picture of a robot.

God always shows love and mercy. As images of God, we should try to show love and mercy.

Directions: Draw a picture of how you have shown love and mercy.

Lesson 2 : God Always Loves Us

We have wills and sometimes we are tempted to do what is wrong. When we know something is wrong and choose to do it anyway, this is a sin. God still loves us, even when we sin. God always forgives us and helps us to do what is right.

Directions: Can you find these words?

ORIGINAL SIN   **TEMPTATION**   **CHOICES**
GRACE   **MERCY**   **SIN**

E	C	J	C	O	X	G	R	A	C	E	Z	T	P
K	H	D	D	R	B	K	P	O	H	O	Y	E	W
T	O	P	D	V	Q	N	V	A	N	N	S	T	M
X	I	C	N	O	J	I	P	I	L	S	G	O	E
W	C	J	D	F	I	M	R	L	G	G	Q	I	R
T	E	M	P	T	A	T	I	O	N	H	L	B	C
X	S	F	B	Q	T	K	T	R	I	N	I	T	Y
S	P	M	L	Q	A	W	S	I	N	V	I	O	P
B	I	V	C	X	L	L	N	G	M	N	J	Z	O
Z	Y	Q	M	F	J	B	C	I	M	V	M	Z	X
L	S	O	G	O	R	O	Q	N	D	D	T	G	U
L	Q	K	S	Y	I	L	C	A	H	L	T	L	W
W	G	C	K	G	R	I	E	L	L	R	H	X	M
E	K	C	S	V	C	W	X	S	A	O	N	J	Y
I	Q	L	O	T	K	A	K	I	W	M	Y	P	F
U	X	V	L	I	T	N	F	N	R	S	H	K	H

Unit 2:   JESUS COMES FOR US

Lesson 3: Jesus, Our Example

God promised Adam and Eve a Savior. Jesus Christ, God the Son, is our Savior. He is the perfect image of God the Father. God the Son became man to show us who we are and how we should act as images of God, to return God's love, and to help us return God's love.

As a young boy, Jesus showed His love by obeying Mary and Joseph. He also showed His love by caring for other people and doing things for them.

How can a family act like the Holy Family?

Directions: The left side of this page and the next page have pictures showing how Jesus, Mary, and Joseph acted. On the right side draw a picture in the spaces provided showing how a family can act like the Holy Family.

Jesus, Mary, and Joseph prayed together.

A family can pray together. Draw a picture of a family praying together.

Lesson 3: Jesus, Our Example

Joseph taught Jesus carpentry.

People in a family teach each other. Draw a picture of someone in a family teaching someone how to do something.

Mary cared for Jesus.

People in a family care for each other. Draw a picture of how a family cares for each other.

Jesus cares for other people.

I care for other people. Draw a picture of how you care for other people.

Lesson 3: Jesus, Our Example

The Baptism of Jesus

A man called John the Baptist lived in the desert near the Jordan River. His clothes were made of camel's hair. John ate grasshoppers and honey.

Many people went to see John. John told the people that the Savior was coming. John told them to get ready for the Savior by being sorry for their sins and by trying not to sin anymore.

In the River Jordan, John baptized the people who were sorry for their sins. These people wanted to change their lives and to try to do better.

One day, Jesus came to the Jordan River to be baptized by John. After John baptized Jesus, God the Holy Spirit came down from heaven like a dove and rested above Jesus. God the Father said that Jesus was His Son whom He loved very much. John believed that Jesus was the Savior.

Then Jesus went into the desert to pray.

Lesson 4: Jesus, Our Teacher

We have read the stories of "The Mission of the Apostles" (Matthew 9:35–38), "Jesus Teaches Us to Pray" (Matthew 6:5–15), "The Wedding at Cana" (John 2:1–12), "The Cure of the Centurion's Servant" (Luke 7:1–10 and Matthew 8:5–13), and the "Parable of the Sower" (Luke 8:4–15 and Matthew 13:1–9, 18–23).

My favorite story is _____

Directions: Draw a picture of your favorite story in the space below.

Lesson 4: Jesus, Our Teacher

Directions: Match the word with its meaning. Draw a line from the vocabulary word to its correct meaning.

Parable

An act which shows the power of God and helps people to have faith in what Jesus taught and helps them to follow Him.

Disciple

A simple story teaching a religious lesson.

Apostles

Holy.

Miracle

A follower of Jesus.

Hallowed

A plant or shrub with thorns.

Trespasses

Twelve friends called by Jesus to follow Him. They answered His call to follow Him by teaching others about Him and by doing His work in a special way.

Brier

A feeling of sharing someone else's suffering along with a choice to help.

Compassion

Sins against God and others.

Jesus' Arrest and Crucifixion

After the Last Supper, Jesus and the Apostles went to a garden. Jesus wanted to pray. Jesus knew what was going to happen. Soon some soldiers came to the garden. They were going to arrest Jesus. One of the Apostles tried to help Jesus. He picked up a sword and cut off one of the soldier's ears.

Jesus knew He would do God the Father's will. Jesus told the Apostle to put the sword away. Then Jesus healed the man's ear.

Jesus was then arrested and led away. The soldiers beat Jesus and made fun of Him.

Jesus was then given the cross. He had to carry it to a place outside the city.

Then the soldiers nailed Jesus to the cross.

Jesus prayed that His Father would forgive the soldiers.

Jesus asked the Apostle, John, to take care of Mary, His Mother.

Then Jesus died.

Lesson 5: Jesus, Our Savior

To _____ means to put someone to death on a cross.

Jesus' death on the cross was a _____ because He offered Himself to God the Father to show His love.

When you fix something, you _____ it.

A share in God's life is called _____.

If you _____ something, you will have to repair it.

Jesus Christ is our _____.

Lesson 5: Jesus, Our Savior

Directions: To show your love, do five sacrifices, and write them next to the numbers 1 through 5. After doing five sacrifices, have your teacher and a parent sign your paper. Then you may color the badge, cut it out, and wear it.

To show my love, I have done these sacrifices.

1. _____

2. _____

3. _____

4. _____

5. _____

X _____ X _____
      Parent's signature   Teacher's signature

Unit 3:   JESUS IS
ALWAYS WITH US

Lesson 6: The Church

Jesus Leaves Us Leaders

One day after eating a meal together, Jesus and Peter were talking.
Jesus said to Peter, "Do you love Me?"
"Yes, Lord," Peter said, "I love You."
Jesus said to Peter, "Feed My lambs."
Jesus asked Peter again, "Do you love Me?"
"Yes, Lord," Peter said, "You know that I love You."
Jesus said, "Tend My sheep."
A third time Jesus asked Peter, "Do you love Me?"
Peter said, "Lord, You know everything. You know that I love You."
Jesus said to Peter, "Feed My sheep."

A shepherd takes care of sheep so they do not get lost and cold or hurt. Jesus made Peter the first leader of the Church. Peter was the first Pope. Peter would guide, love, and care for the Church, just like a good shepherd would take care of his sheep. The other Apostles helped Peter.

The Church loves and cares for us the way Jesus loves and cares for us. The Church teaches us what Jesus taught and helps us know how to act as images of God so that we may be happy here on earth and one day in heaven.

Lesson 6: The Church

community

Pope

parish

bishops

Church

witness

1. The _____ is the man who takes Peter's place today and serves as the leader of the Catholic Church on earth.

2. A _____ is the church community that we belong to.

3. A person who has seen or heard something is a _____

4. People who believe in Jesus Christ and follow His teachings are called _____

5. A _____ is someone who is a Christian and belongs to the Catholic Church.

6. A group of people who love each other and share the same beliefs and interests are a _____

7. The _____ are men who teach the people how to act as images of God the way the Apostles did.

8. The _____ are men who have answered God's call and have chosen to offer their lives to Him and act as helpers to the bishop.

Catholic

Christians

priests

Lesson 6: The Church

A play is not just a stage. You need an author to write the play. You need actors and actresses to act out the play. You need a director to tell the actors and actresses what to do. You need people to watch the play. All of these people join together to make one play.

When we were baptized, we became members of the Catholic Church. Jesus Christ, the Holy Spirit, and all the baptized are joined together to make one Church. Jesus is the leader of the Church. The Holy Spirit guides the Church. The Pope is the leader of the Church on earth. The Pope and the bishops carry on the work of Jesus. As members of the Church, we help care for the other members of the Church all over the world.

Directions: Look at the next two pages. On one page there is a picture of a stage. On the other page are pictures of members of the Church. Color the stage. Then color the pictures of the members of the Church. Cut out the pictures and glue them onto the paper stage.

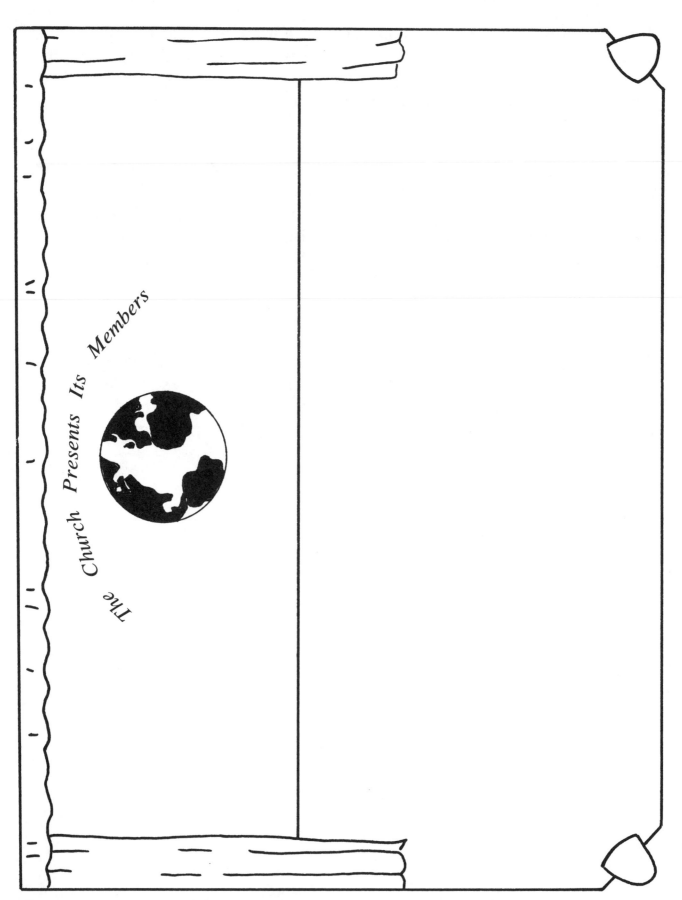

The Church Presents Its Members

Lesson 6: The Church

Lesson 7: We Meet Jesus in the Sacraments

Jesus lived on the earth almost 2,000 years ago. Jesus is God, but He is also a man. When He was on earth, Jesus could use His senses. Jesus told people about God's love. Jesus looked lovingly at people with His eyes. He listened to people with His ears. Jesus touched people with His hands.

When Jesus returned to heaven, He gave us sacraments to help us. These sacraments are physical signs that Jesus gave us so that we can meet Jesus and receive His grace. Jesus loved and touched people 2,000 years ago. Now, Jesus loves us and touches us through the sacraments. Jesus gives us grace so that we are able to love God and others here on earth and someday in heaven.

We receive the sacraments through the Church. The deacons, priests, and bishops act for Jesus. When the deacon, priest, or bishop celebrates a sacrament, it is really Jesus Who is giving us the sacrament.

Lesson 7: We Meet Jesus in the Sacraments

Jesus often talked to sick people and healed them. Jesus showed His love and compassion for a leper and a blind man. Jesus reached out and touched these people with His hands and cured them.

Jesus touched people in another way. Jesus touched their hearts with His words. Jesus showed His love and compassion for people when they made a wrong choice and was willing to forgive their sins.

Sarah

One day, many people were in the temple listening to what Jesus was teaching. The Pharisees brought a woman named Sarah to Jesus. She had been caught making a wrong choice on purpose. They wanted to punish Sarah by throwing stones at her. Jesus did not answer them. The Pharisees kept questioning Jesus. Finally Jesus said to them, "Let the man among you who has no sin be the first to cast a stone at her."

At this, the people began to walk away, because they remembered wrong choices they had made. Finally, only Jesus and Sarah were left. Jesus asked Sarah where all the people went. Jesus asked Sarah if anyone had decided to punish her. Sarah said, "No one, Sir." Jesus told Sarah that He would not punish her either, but He asked Sarah not to make this wrong choice again.

Jesus showed His love and compassion for Sarah and did not punish her.

Lesson 7: We Meet Jesus in the Sacraments

Jesus loves us and touches us through the seven sacraments. The seven sacraments are: Baptism, Confirmation, Holy Eucharist, Reconciliation, Matrimony, Holy Orders, and Anointing of the Sick.

Directions: Can you match each sacrament with the correct picture? Write the name of the sacrament on the line under the matching picture.

Baptism

Holy Orders

Confirmation

39

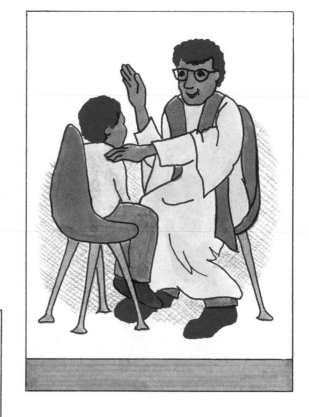

Reconciliation
Anointing of the Sick
Holy Eucharist
Matrimony

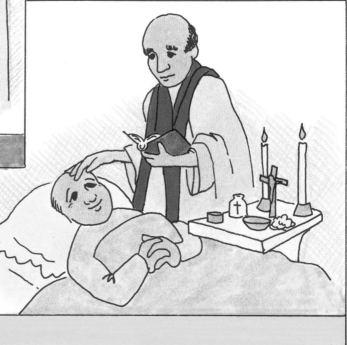

Lesson 8: We Receive New Life

Directions: Fill in the blanks in the following sentences using the words listed in the word box.

baptized	images of God	grace
faith	promises	
heaven	God	sign	candle	God's

1. We join God's family when we are _____ .

2. We receive _____ that helps us to act as images of God.

3. Our parents and godparents make _____for us. They promise to help us act as _____ .

4. When we are baptized, we receive the gift of _____ . This gift helps us believe in _____ and to believe that if we follow Jesus, we will be able to share life in _____ with Him.

5. We receive a _____ to remind us that Jesus shows us the way; He is our light.

6. A white garment is a _____ that we have received new life, _____ life.

Lesson 8: We Receive New Life

Directions: Color the pictures on this page and the next page. Cut out the pictures and arrange them on a piece of construction paper. Do not put them too closely together. Cut out the words or phrases from the page that follows the pictures, and place them on the construction paper by the proper picture. When the pictures and words or phrases are arranged correctly, glue them in place onto the construction paper. Write the word BAPTISM on the top of the construction paper.

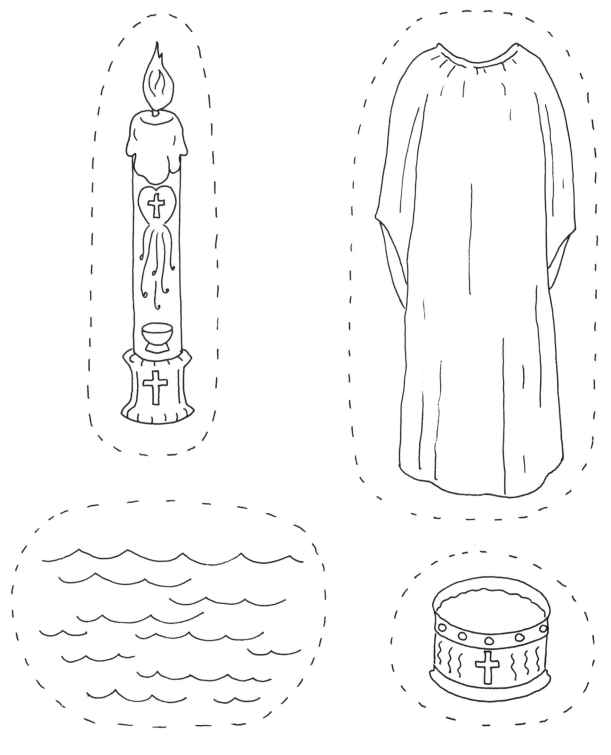

Lesson 8: We Receive New Life

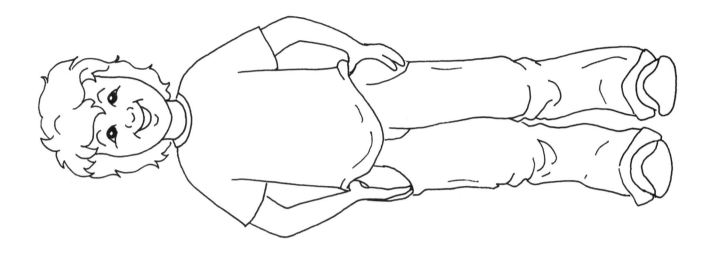

Lesson 8: We Receive New Life

Directions: Cut out the words or phrases from this page and place them on the construction paper by the proper picture. (See more detailed directions on the previous pages.)

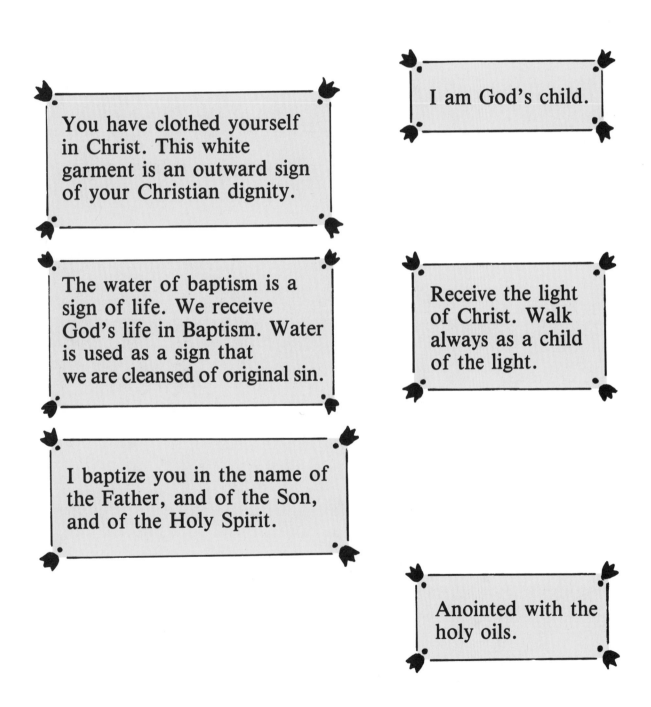

You have clothed yourself in Christ. This white garment is an outward sign of your Christian dignity.

I am God's child.

The water of baptism is a sign of life. We receive God's life in Baptism. Water is used as a sign that we are cleansed of original sin.

Receive the light of Christ. Walk always as a child of the light.

I baptize you in the name of the Father, and of the Son, and of the Holy Spirit.

Anointed with the holy oils.

Unit 4:   WE LEARN TO ACT
AS IMAGES OF GOD

Abraham and Isaac

A long time ago God wanted to give Abraham a chance to love Him. God asked Abraham to offer his son, Isaac, to Him. Abraham loved his son very much, and this would be very hard for Abraham to do.

Abraham loved God more than any other person. God was more important to Abraham than anything else. Abraham trusted God and was ready to do what God asked.

Just as Abraham was ready to offer Isaac to God, God sent an angel to stop him because Abraham had shown that he loved God even more than his son.

God loves and cares for us. God wants us to love Him more than any other person. God should be more important to us than anything else.

Moses

A long time ago there was a good man named Moses. God asked Moses to be the leader of His people, the Israelites, who were slaves in Egypt.

Moses led God's people across the desert to a mountain called Sinai. Moses went up to the top of the mountain. Moses was on the mountain with God for many days. God gave him the Ten Commandments written on two stone tablets.

The people got tired of waiting for Moses and forgot how God loved and cared for them. They decided to make themselves a new god. They melted their gold jewelry and made a golden calf and sang and danced around it.

When Moses came down the mountain and saw what the people had done, he was very angry. He threw down the stone tablets and broke them. He destroyed the golden calf.

Moses went back up the mountain and prayed for the people. God told Moses to make two new stone tablets and write the Ten Commandments on them. Moses did what God asked.

Moses took the two tablets down the mountain to the Israelites. He told them about the Ten Commandments. Moses told them that these were the ways they should act as images of God.

Lesson 9: We Love God

God gave us Ten Commandments that tell us how we should love God and how we should love others. They tell us how to act as images of God and come to heaven.

Circle the picture where the person or persons, by keeping the first three commandments, are loving God as they should and are acting as images of God.

1. **"I, the Lord, am your God, you will not have other gods besides Me."**

Joe is so busy with other things every day that he doesn't make time for God.

Jane remembers that all things are gifts from God and that she should love God more than any person or thing. Jane takes time each day to tell God thank you.

2. "You will not take the name of the Lord your God in vain."

Cathy uses bad words and calls Bill names.

Dan talks about God and tells his parents what he learned about being an image of God.

3. "Remember to keep holy the sabbath day."

Karen and Eric go to Mass each Sunday. They listen carefully to God's word.

Scott and Sue were up late and decided to sleep late and not go to Mass.

54

Lesson 9: We Love God

Directions: Write the answers to each of the statements on the lines provided. The answers may be found in the word box.

commandments

sacrifice

Sabbath

Moses

false

Isaac

Abraham

Across

1. The way God acts and the way God wants us to act as His images. _____

3. Not true. _____

5. An action where someone or something is offered to God as a sign of love. _____

6. Abraham's son. _____

Down

2. The Lord's day. _____

4. This man showed God how much he loved Him. _____

7. God gave this man the Ten Commandments. _____

VOCABULARY WORDS:

Commandment: The way God acts and the way God wants us to act as His images.

Sabbath: The Lord's day, the day we go to church.

False: Not true.

Sacrifice: An action where someone or something is offered to God as a sign of love.

BREAD OF LIFE

Recipe:
Loving God

Made by: _____

1. _____
2. _____
3. _____
4. _____
5. _____
6. _____
7. _____

Do these each day to help you be a better image of God.

Lesson 9 : We Love God

Ten Commandments Booklet

This booklet tells you each of the commandments, and what each commandment means. There are also some questions to ask yourself to see if you are keeping the commandments and are acting as an image of God. These questions are called an Examination of Conscience.

To make this booklet you will need to do the following:

1. *Find pages 61 through 81 in your book.*

2. *Remove these pages from your book.*

3. *Put the pages in order by number with page 61 on top. The pages are numbered 61 through 81.*

4. *Get two pieces of construction paper from your teacher. Put one piece of construction paper on top of the Ten Commandments pages to make a front cover for your booklet. Put the other piece of construction paper behind the Ten Commandments pages to make a back cover for your booklet.*

5. *Staple the Ten Commandments booklet together along the left-hand side of the booklet.*

6. *On the front cover of your booklet write* The Ten Commandments *as a title for your booklet.*

7. *On the back of pages 63 through 81, draw a picture of yourself showing how you are keeping each commandment. (For example, on the back of page 63, draw a picture of yourself keeping the first commandment.)*

Lesson 9: We Love God

Ten Commandments Booklet

1. I, the Lord, am your God, you will not have other gods besides Me.

2. You will not take the name of the Lord your God in vain.

3. Remember to keep holy the sabbath day.

4. Honor your father and your mother.

5. You will not kill.

6. You will not commit adultery.

7. You will not steal.

8. You will not bear false witness against your neighbor.

9. You will not covet your neighbor's wife.

10. You will not covet anything that belongs to your neighbor.

Ten Commandments Booklet

Some questions I should ask myself.

Do I tell God I love Him and thank Him for all He has given me?

Is there any thing that has become so important to me that I forget God?

Do I pray every day?

First Commandment:

1. I, the Lord, am your God, you will not have other gods besides Me.

What this commandment means:

This commandment tells me that I should love God more than any other person. God should be more important to me than anything.

Ten Commandments Booklet

Some questions I should ask myself.

Do I use God's name in a loving way?

Do I use other people's names in a loving way?

Do I use bad words?

Second Commandment:

2. You will not take the name of the Lord your God in vain.

What this commandment means:

This commandment tells me that I should use God's name with love and respect.

Ten Commandments Booklet

Some questions I should ask myself.

Do I go to Mass on Sundays and Holy Days?

Do I pay attention when I am at Mass?

Do I listen carefully?

Do I behave the way I should when I am in the church?

Third Commandment:

3. Remember to keep holy the sabbath day.

What this commandment means:

This commandment tells me that I should go to Mass on God's days (Sundays and Holy Days) to celebrate God's love for us and remember everything God has done for us.

Ten Commandments Booklet

Some questions I should ask myself.

Do I listen to my parents and others who take care of me?

Do I respect my parents and follow the rules they have made for my safety and good?

Do I help my parents at home by doing the jobs they ask me to do?

Do I show my love for my parents?

Fourth Commandment:

4. Honor your father and your mother.

What this commandment means:

This commandment tells me I should listen to, respect, and love my parents and those people who take care of me when I am not with my parents (teachers, grandparents, and priests, for example).

Ten Commandments Booklet

Some questions I should ask myself.

Do I treat other people with kindness and respect?

Do I help other people when I can?

Do I hurt others' feelings by name-calling or making fun of them?

Do I care for myself by eating the proper food and getting enough sleep and exercise?

Do I hit anyone?

Do I fight with anyone?

Fifth Commandment:

5. You will not kill.

What this commandment means:

This commandment tells me I should treat other people with love and respect. I should care for myself and help care for other people.

Ten Commandments Booklet

Some questions I should ask myself.

Do I respect the privacy of the members of my family?

Do I knock at a closed door before entering?

Do I close the door when I am using the bathroom?

Do I close the door when I am in the bedroom dressing?

Sixth Commandment:
6. You will not commit adultery.

What this commandment means:
This commandment tells me that a husband and wife should be loyal to each other. They have a special love that they share only with each other.

This commandment also tells me that I should respect the privacy of other people.

Ten Commandments Booklet

Some questions I should ask myself.

Do I take money or other things that are not mine?

If I find money or some other thing in my classroom or at home do I try to find out to whom it belongs?

When I want to borrow something, do I ask the person to whom it belongs if I may borrow it?

Do I take good care of the things that I borrow, and do I return them when I am done using them?

Seventh Commandment:

7. You will not steal.

What this commandment means:

This commandment tells me that I should never take what does not belong to me.

If I borrow something I should take good care of it and return it when I am done using it.

Lesson 9: We Love God

Ten Commandments Booklet

Some questions I should ask myself.

Do I always tell the truth?

Do I say mean things about other people?

Do I hurt other people by telling lies about them?

Eighth Commandment:
8. You will not bear false witness against your neighbor.

What this commandment means:
This commandment tells me that I should always tell the truth. I should only say good things about other people. I should not tell lies about other people.

Ten Commandments Booklet

Some questions I should ask myself.

Do I want to have my friend's parents because they let my friend do things my parents will not let me do?

Am I happy with the friends that I have?

Am I happy with the family God has given me?

Ninth Commandment:

9. You will not covet your neighbor's wife.

What this commandment means:

This commandment tells me that I should be happy with the special people God has given me in my life. I should not be envious and want someone else's family or friends.

Ten Commandments Booklet

Some questions I should ask myself.

Am I happy with the things that I have?

Am I happy for others when they get something that I want?

Am I happy for others when something good happens to them?

Tenth Commandment:
10. You will not covet anything that belongs to your neighbor.

What this commandment means:
This commandment tells me that I should be happy with the things that I have and not be envious if someone else has something that I want.

Good Samaritan

Daniel was walking along a road. He was robbed and hurt, and left on the side of the road. Two men saw that Daniel needed help. They did not stop to help him. James saw Daniel. James did not know Daniel but he stopped. He gave Daniel some water and helped make him feel better. James took Daniel to an inn and paid for his care.

Jesus told this story. He told us so that we would know that everyone is our neighbor. We should love and care for everyone just as we want to be loved and cared for.

Directions: Finish the picture.

Lesson 10: We Love Others

Directions: Here are the Ten Commandments. They are missing some words. Using the words in the tablets, can you complete each commandment?

1. I, the _____ , am your _____ , you will not have other gods besides me.

2. You will not take the _____ of the Lord your God in _____ .

3. Remember to keep _____ the sabbath day.

4. _____ your father and your mother.

5. You will not _____ .

6. You will not commit _____ .

7. You will not _____ .

8. You will not bear false witness against your _____ .

9. You will not _____ your neighbor's wife.

10. You will not covet anything that belongs to your _____ .

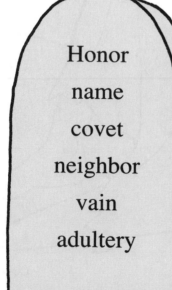

Honor

name

covet

neighbor

vain

adultery

God

steal

holy

kill

neighbor

Lord

Lesson 10: We Love Others

BREAD OF LIFE

Recipe:
Loving Others

Made by _____

1. _____

2. _____

3. _____

4. _____

5. _____

6. _____

7. _____

Do these each day to help you be a better image of God

Lesson 11: Sin

Directions: Look at the pictures below. Some of the pictures show right choices, and some show wrong choices. A wrong choice made on purpose is a sin. Mark an X by each picture showing a wrong choice. Color each picture showing a right choice.

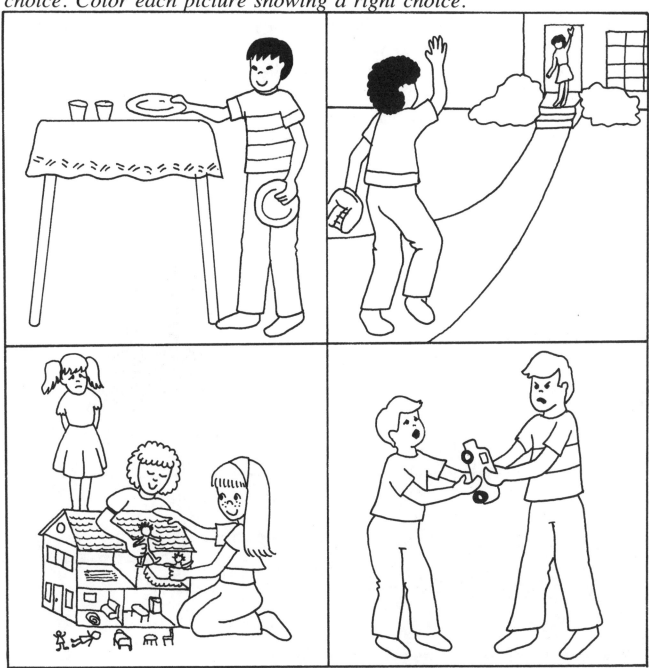

Directions: Match each word with its meaning.

sin   sorry

When you know something is wrong but you choose to do it anyway. You are not acting as an image of God should. _____

When you feel unhappy for making wrong choices. _____

Lesson 11: Sin

Sinful Woman

Jesus was having dinner at Simon's house. A woman who had lived a sinful life came to visit Him. She was sorry for making wrong choices. When she saw Jesus, she began to cry. She washed His feet with her tears and dried His feet with her hair. Then she covered Jesus' feet with perfume. Jesus knew she was sorry for her sins. He forgave her sins and told her to go in peace.

Unit 5:   GOD ALWAYS LOVES US

Lesson 12: God Is Our Loving Father

Directions: In the space below, draw a picture of the younger son spending his money on the things he thinks will make him happy.

The Story of the Prodigal Son

There was a man who had two sons. The younger son wanted his share of the money so that he could have some fun and be on his own.

The father gave his younger son the money. The younger son took the money and went to another country. He spent all his money on the things he thought would make him happy.

Lesson 12: God Is Our Loving Father

Then there was a famine in that country and there was not much food. The boy was very hungry. He had no place to live and all of his money was gone.

The boy found a job taking care of some pigs. The boy was so hungry, but no one gave him any food to eat.

The boy was sorry he left his father who loved him. The boy decided to go back home to his father and tell him he was sorry for the wrong he had done.

Lesson 12: God Is Our Loving Father

The boy's father was sad when his son had gone away and was worried about him. Every morning he went down the road and looked, hoping his son would come home.

One morning when the father went down the road he saw a boy in ragged clothes walking along the road toward him. The father saw that the boy was his younger son. While his son was still a long way from home, his father ran to meet him. The boy told his father he was sorry.

The boy's father was happy his son had come home. He hugged and kissed him. He was happy to forgive his son. They had a big party.

Lesson 12: God Is Our Loving Father

Directions: In the space below, draw a picture of the father talking with his older son.

The older son returned home from working in the field. He was angry that they were having a party for his brother after his brother had wasted his father's money.

The father went out to his older son and told him, "You are with me always, and all I have is yours. You should be happy that your younger brother has returned home to be with us."

Lesson 12: God Is Our Loving Father

Directions: Finish the sentence by matching the correct answer in column B with column A.

A

_____1. The loving and forgiving father is like

_____2. When we make a wrong choice and are sorry we are like the

_____3. When we tell God we are sorry, He

_____4. As images of God, we should forgive

_____5. The younger son spent all his money on things

B

a. Prodigal Son.

b. forgives us.

c. God.

d. he thought would make him happy.

e. others.

Lesson 12: God Is Our Loving Father

As images of God we should forgive others in the same way God forgives us. We need to forgive the wrong that was done to us and not stay angry or hurt. When we forgive someone, we are loving that person.

Directions: Draw a line under the pictures that show forgiveness.

God is our loving and forgiving Father. God loves us even when we sin, but the sin weakens the love between God and us. God forgives us when we tell Him we are sorry and brings us closer to Him.

God is my loving Father, God forgives me when I tell Him I am sorry.

VOCABULARY WORDS:

Forgive: To go on loving a person who has hurt us and to let go of the hurt or angry feelings.

Sorrow: A feeling of sadness over an action that has hurt someone.

Famine: A lot of people not having enough food for a long time.

Directions: Can you find the following words that are hidden in the puzzle?

FORGIVE   MAKE UP   SORROW   FAMINE
FATHER   LOVE   PRODIGAL SON

P	A	K	W	Y	Q	M	C	H	S	D
R	P	E	Q	O	N	A	L	T	B	F
O	C	G	J	M	P	K	S	V	X	A
D	Z	F	A	T	H	E	R	U	W	M
I	J	O	K	N	C	U	T	Q	A	I
G	L	R	D	E	G	P	B	C	H	N
A	M	G	F	P	N	Y	L	O	Q	E
L	P	I	X	A	S	O	R	R	O	W
S	T	V	I	O	M	U	Z	W	A	E
O	C	E	D	H	S	N	O	T	A	L
N	G	L	O	V	E	P	M	D	K	T

Lesson 13: Sacrament of Reconciliation

When we love God, we admit our sins, and are sorry for our sins.

Jesus gave us the Sacrament of Reconciliation so that we can tell Him our sins and receive His forgiveness.

In the Sacrament of Reconciliation the priest acts for Jesus. When we tell the priest our sins and say we are sorry, we are really telling Jesus.

When the priest says the words of forgiveness, it is Jesus Who forgives us—Jesus Who heals us. Jesus gives us His grace to help us return God's love and to help us make right choices in the future.

We can tell Jesus we are sorry for our sins, and receive His forgiveness in the Sacrament of Reconciliation.

Lesson 13 : Sacrament of Reconcilation

When we are sick with a bad cold, we go to a doctor for help. The doctor gives us medicine so we feel better. When our tooth hurts, we go to the dentist for help. The dentist puts a filling in our tooth to save it.

When we sin, we hurt God, ourselves and others. Our sins weaken our love for God. We wound ourselves, we hurt others. When we hurt because of the unloving choices we have made, we go to Jesus for help in the Sacrament of Reconciliation. When we tell our sins to the priest, we are telling Jesus. We receive Jesus' forgiveness. Jesus heals the wounds of our sins. He gives us grace that helps us love God and others as we should.

Directions: Match the "hurt" or "problem" with the one that "helps" or "heals" it.

Lesson 13: Sacrament of Reconciliation

The Good Shepherd

There was a shepherd who had one hundred sheep that he loved and took care of. One day the shepherd lost one of his sheep. The shepherd worried about his lost sheep because he knew the sheep might get cold or hurt or attacked by hungry wolves.

The shepherd left the other sheep safe together. He looked for the lost sheep because he wanted to help the sheep return home. The shepherd had to be very careful because he could get cold or hurt or attacked by the hungry wolves too.

When the shepherd found his lost sheep he was so happy that he picked the sheep up and carried it all the way home. The shepherd told all his friends he found his lost sheep and everyone was so happy!

Jesus is the Good Shepherd and we are His sheep. Sometimes we sin and are like the lost sheep. Jesus our Good Shepherd helps us to return to Him through the Sacrament of Reconciliation.

Lesson 13: Sacrament of Reconciliation

Directions: Help the Good Shepherd find his way through the maze and get to his lost sheep.

Lesson 13: Sacrament of Reconciliation

Vocabulary Words:

Reconciliation: To reconcile; to rebuild the friendship between persons.

Sacrament: 1. Is a physical sign,
2. given to us by Jesus,
3. through which Jesus meets us
4. and gives us grace.

Shepherd: One who takes care of sheep.

Crucify: To put to death on a cross.

Contrition: Sorrow for our sins.

Act of Contrition: A prayer that tells God we are sorry for our sins because we have hurt Him, ourselves, and others and that with His help we will try not to sin again.

My God,
I am sorry for my sins
with all my heart.
In choosing to do wrong
and failing to do good,
I have sinned against You
Whom I should love above all things.
I have hurt myself and others.
I firmly intend, with Your help,
to do penance,
to sin no more,
and to avoid whatever leads me
to sin.
Our Savior Jesus Christ
suffered and died for us.
In His name, my God, have mercy.

Lesson 14: How We Receive the Sacrament of Reconciliation

When we love God, we admit our sins. We are sorry for our sins because they hurt God, ourselves and others. We receive the healing touch of Jesus in the Sacrament of Reconciliation. In the Sacrament of Reconciliation, our sins are forgiven.

Before we receive the Sacrament of Reconciliation, we need to take time and ask ourselves if we have been acting as images of God and how we can act as better images of God. We ask ourselves if we have been following the Ten Commandments, and how we can follow them even better. We think of the sins we have done. When we ask ourselves if we have been following the Ten Commandments we are making an Examination of Conscience.

Use your Ten Commandments Booklet to help you make a good Examination of Conscience before you receive the Sacrament of Reconciliation.

VOCABULARY WORDS:

Penance: A loving act which the priest asks us to do after our sins have been forgiven.

Absolution: The words spoken by the priest which take away our sins.

Act of contrition: A prayer that tells God we are sorry for our sins because we have hurt Him, ourselves, and others and that with His help we will try not to sin again.

Confession: Telling the priest our sins.

Absolve: To take away.

Examination of conscience: By using the Ten Commandments we take time to ask ourselves if we have been acting as images of God and how we should act as better images of God.

Lesson 14: How We Receive the Sacrament of Reconciliation

Suggested Form for Receiving the Sacrament of Reconciliation

1. Make a good Examination of Conscience. Be ready to tell the priest your sins.

2. Go into the confessional and kneel down, or go into the reconciliation room and sit/kneel down. Greet the priest.

3. Make the "Sign of the Cross" and say, "Father, I have sinned. This is my first confession."
   (For all other confessions, tell the priest how long it has been since your last confession.)

4. Tell the priest your sins. When you are done, say, "I am very sorry for all my sins."

5. The priest will talk with you and will help you find ways to be more loving to God and others.

6. The priest will give you a penance.

7. The priest will ask you to say an Act of Contrition.

8. The priest will give you absolution. Listen carefully so you can hear the words of forgiveness and so you know when to make the "Sign of the Cross" and answer "Amen."

9. The priest will say "Go in peace." Thank the priest and leave the confessional or reconciliation room.

10. Do your penance *right away*.

Lesson 14: How We Receive the Sacrament of Reconciliation

Here are steps to making a good confession.
Put them in the correct order.

_____ I say I am sorry for all my sins.

_____ I receive a penance.

_____ I greet the priest.

_____ I thank the priest.

_____ I say the Act of Contrition.

_____ I tell the priest my sins.

_____ I listen to the priest tell me how to be a more loving person.

_____ The priest gives me absolution.

_____ I make a good Examination of Conscience.

_____ I do my penance.

Unit 6:   JESUS GIVES US LIVING BREAD

Lesson 15: Jesus Is the Bread of Life

Multiplication of the Loaves and Fish

One time when Jesus was by the Sea of Galilee with His disciples, a very large crowd of about 5,000 people came to listen to Him. Jesus told them about God the Father and heaven. Jesus healed the people who were sick. The people stayed with Jesus the whole day and were very hungry when evening came. Jesus asked the disciples what food there was to feed the people. One of the disciples named Andrew found a boy who had five loaves of bread and two fish. The boy gave the bread and fish to Jesus. Jesus told the disciples to have the people sit down. Then Jesus took the loaves of bread and the fish. Jesus looked up to heaven and gave thanks to God the Father. Jesus broke the loaves of bread into pieces. Jesus asked His disciples to give the bread and fish to the people. There was enough bread and fish for everyone to eat! Jesus had taken five loaves of bread and two fish, and He made enough to feed 5,000 people! After everyone had eaten, Jesus asked His disciples to collect the food left over. There were twelve full baskets of food left!

Lesson 15: Jesus Is the Bread of Life

Jesus asked His disciples to pick up all the leftover food and put it in baskets.

Directions: Number the baskets to find out how many were filled after the 5,000 people had eaten of the 5 loaves of bread and 2 fish that Jesus had blessed.

How many baskets of food were left? _____

Lesson 15: Jesus Is the Bread of Life

God's life in us needs to grow strong. Jesus helps God's life to grow strong by giving us Living Bread. Jesus is our Bread of Life. Jesus is present for us in the Sacrament of the Holy Eucharist. The Holy Eucharist is the Body and Blood of Jesus.

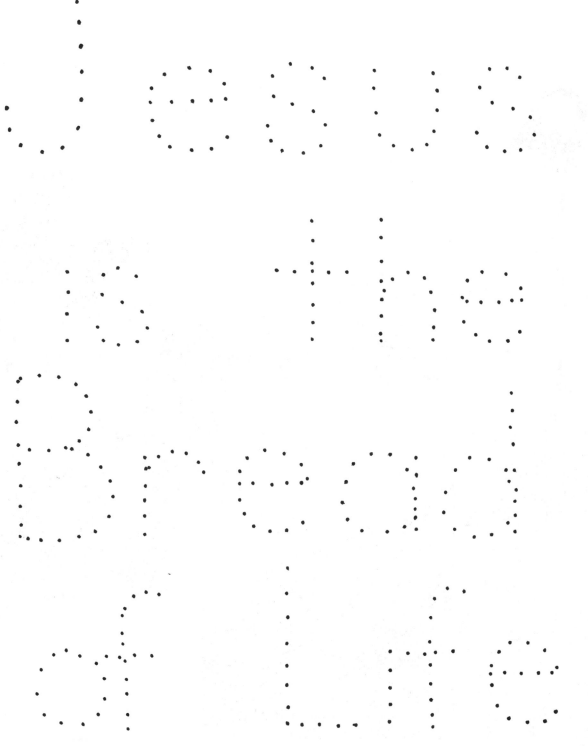

Lesson 15: Jesus Is the Bread of Life

Directions: Write what happens in this story in your own words.

_____

_____

_____

_____

_____

Vocabulary Words

Faith   Disciples

Miracle   Apostles

Lesson 16: Jesus Shares a Special Meal

The chosen people were slaves in Egypt. The chosen people wanted to leave Egypt. Moses asked the King of Egypt to let them leave. The King would not let them go. As long as the chosen people were slaves, God allowed plagues to trouble the people of Egypt.

God talked to Moses about one last plague that would change the King's mind. God asked the chosen people to kill a young lamb and put some of the lamb's blood on the door frames of their houses. God asked them to eat a meal of roasted lamb, a bitter herb salad and unleavened bread. The chosen people did what God asked.

That night God allowed the firstborn son of every family to die, except in the houses that had the door frame marked with lamb's blood. God allowed the plague to pass over the chosen people. Their sons did not die. God saved the chosen people from this last plague because they did what God asked. They accepted God's loving care.

The next day the chosen people were allowed to leave Egypt.

Directions: Draw a picture of the special meal that Moses and the people ate.

Lesson 16: Jesus Shares a Special Meal

People waved palm branches at Jesus on _____ _____ .

Jesus turned the bread into His Body and the wine into His Blood for the first time at the _____ _____

The _____ is celebrated so that people remember the time God allowed the Israelites to be spared the final plague.

A _____ causes great trouble or misery.

The Jewish people learned about the rules from the _____ .

Lesson 16: Jesus Shares a Special Meal

The Last Supper

Jesus and His Apostles went to Jerusalem to share the Passover meal together in a large room. During the meal, Jesus washed and dried the feet of His Apostles to show them how they should serve each other and other people.

Then Jesus did something very special. Jesus took the bread, blessed it, saying, ''THIS IS MY BODY'', and it became His Body. Then He gave it to His Apostles to eat.

Jesus took the cup of wine, blessed it, saying, ''THIS IS THE CUP OF MY BLOOD'', and it became His Blood. Jesus gave the cup to His Apostles to drink.

This special meal is called the Last Supper.

At Mass, when we go to Holy Communion, we are receiving Jesus' Body and Blood. Jesus loves us so much that He gives Himself to us in the Holy Eucharist.

(Note: Chapter 19 follows.)

Unit 7:   WE ACT AS IMAGES OF GOD

Lesson 19: We Love and Serve God, and Others

Each person has a calling from God to love and to serve Him, and others. Each person has a vocation. Some people have a vocation to Holy Orders or to the religious life in the Catholic Church. These people are priests, deacons, brothers and sisters. They have chosen to answer God's call by devoting their lives to loving and serving God, and others in certain ways.

People who are not priests, deacons, brothers, or sisters have a vocation too. These people love and serve God, and others by being married and raising a family or by living a single life. Single people often do good works such as teaching, visiting the sick, giving medical care to people who are sick, and other good things. Married people may do these good works too.

Sometimes priests, deacons, brothers, sisters, and others love and serve other people in another country or in their own country as missionaries. They bring the love of God to the people. Sometimes they teach the people about Jesus. They help care for the people by giving them food, clothing, and medical care. They show the people how to grow food and how to care for themselves.

Lesson 19: We Love and Serve God, and Others

Directions: Draw a picture of yourself loving and serving God, and others.

Lesson 20: We Talk and Listen to God

Prayer of St. Francis

Lord, make me an instrument of Your peace.
    Where there is hatred, let me sow love;
    where there is injury, pardon;
    where there is doubt, faith;
    where there is despair, hope;
    where there is darkness, light; and
    where there is sadness, joy.

O, divine Master,
grant that I may seek not so much
to be consoled as to console;
to be understood as to understand;
to be loved as to love;
for it is in giving that we receive;
it is in pardoning that we are pardoned;
and it is in dying that we are born
to eternal life.

Amen.

Lesson 20: We Talk and Listen to God

Jesus Prays For Strength

On the night He shared the Last Supper, Jesus and His Apostles went to the Garden of Gethsemani. Jesus was very, very sad. Jesus knew that the soliders and guards would soon come to arrest Him and to crucify Him. Jesus went to a quiet spot in the garden to pray.

Jesus said, "My Father, if it is possible, let this cup pass Me by. Still, let it be as You would have it, not as I." While Jesus was praying, the Apostles fell asleep. They were so tired that they could not keep their eyes open. Jesus returned to the Apostles, and finding them asleep, Jesus went back to the quiet spot and continued to pray.

Jesus was so sad. Jesus told God the Father that He would do what His Father wanted. He prayed that the Father would give Him strength to suffer and to die on the cross. In His great suffering, Jesus prayed very hard. Finally, Jesus returned to His Apostles and woke them up. Then the soldiers and guards came and arrested Jesus.

God always hears and answers our prayers. God does not always answer our prayers the way we want them to be answered. God answers our prayers in the way that He knows is best. When our prayers are not answered the way we want them to be, or, when we need strength to do something that is hard for us to do, we should pray to God the way Jesus did in the Garden of Gethsemani. God the Holy Spirit is always with us to help us and to give us strength.

Lesson 20: We Talk and Listen to God

Prayer is talking to God. When we pray, we raise our minds and hearts to God. We can pray anywhere—at home, at school, in church, on the playground. We can say prayers praising God for His power, wisdom, and love. We can say prayers telling God "Thank You" for all He gives to us. We can ask God for the things we need, and we can tell God we are sorry for our wrong choices, and ask God for His forgiveness.

Our prayers can be short or long. We can pray alone or with other people. St. Francis of Assisi prayed and listened to God. When we pray, we should also take time to be quiet and listen to God. He speaks to us in our hearts. We can have a closer relationship with God by taking time to pray and to listen to Him.

Lesson 20: We Talk and Listen to God

Directions: Remove this page from your book. On the back of the holy card titled "We Thank God for All That He Gives Us", write a prayer telling God "Thank You" for what He has given to you. On the back of the holy card titled "We Ask God for the Things We Need", write a prayer asking God for something that you need. Color the pictures on each holy card. Cut out the holy cards.

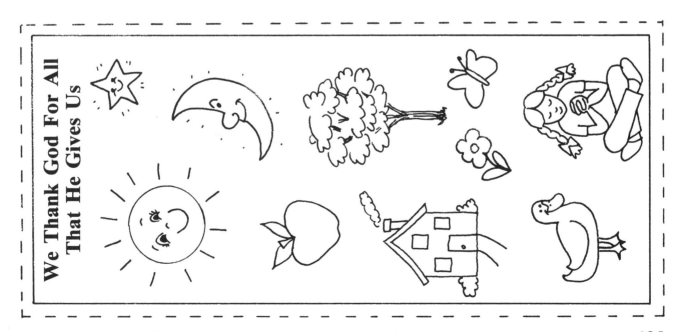

Unit 8: LITURGICAL SEASONS AND HOLIDAYS

Guardian Angel Prayer

Angel of God, my guardian dear,
To whom God's love commits me here,
Ever this day be at my side
to light and to guard,
to rule and guide.　Amen.

Directions: Write your favorite story in your own words.

_____

_____

_____

_____

_____

_____

_____

_____

_____

Lesson 22: Advent

Advent Service

First Week of Advent:

Adult: The first week of Advent, we light one candle as a sign of hope. (Light one purple candle.)

Child: "Your ways, O Lord, make known to me;
teach me Your paths,
Guide me in Your truth and teach me,
for You are God my Savior,
and for You I wait all the day."
(Psalm 25:4-5)

Child: John the Baptist helped people long ago to prepare their hearts for the Savior. O God, help us to prepare our hearts for Jesus, as we wait for His birthday.

Everyone: Come Lord Jesus, and light our way with hope.

Second Week of Advent:

Adult: The second week of Advent we light one candle as a sign of hope, and one candle as a sign of peace. (Light two purple candles.)

Child: "Blest too the peacemakers; they shall be called sons of God."
(Matthew 5:9)

Child: O God, help us to be peacemakers with our families and with our friends even when it is hard to do.

Everyone: Come Lord Jesus and light our way with peace.

Lesson 22: Advent

Third Week of Advent:

Adult: The third week of Advent we light one candle as a sign of hope, one candle as a sign of peace, and one candle as a sign of joy. (Light two purple candles and one pink candle.)

Child: "But I shall see you again;
then your hearts will rejoice with a
joy no one can take from you."
(John 16:22)

Child: Thank You Jesus for being our Savior. Help us to follow You now so that someday we will live with You in heaven.

Everyone: Come Lord Jesus and light our way with joy.

Fourth Week of Advent:

Adult: The fourth week of Advent we light one candle as a sign of hope, one candle as a sign of peace, one candle as a sign of joy, and one candle as a sign of love. (Light all of the candles on the Advent wreath.)

Child: "This is My commandment:
love one another
as I have loved you."
(John 15:12)

Child: Jesus, help me to bring Your love to other people by acting more like You.

Everyone: Come Lord Jesus and light our way with love.

Lesson 22: Advent

Directions: Color the pictures below. Cut out the pictures and arrange them on a red paper heart. Glue them in place.

The Christmas Story (based on Luke 1:26–56, 2:1–19, and Matt 2:1–12)

Characters: Mary, Joseph, Angel Gabriel, three angels, Caesar Augustus, soldier, three wise men (Melchior, Gaspar, Balthasar), King Herod, advisor, three shepherds (Seth, Tim, and Andrew), three innkeepers (Amos, Zach, Michael), Elizabeth, Narrator(s).

Act 1

Narrator: This is a story about something that happened almost 2,000 years ago in the town of Nazareth. There is a young girl whose name is Mary. She is engaged to a man named Joseph. One night, God sends the angel Gabriel to Mary with a message.

Angel Gabriel: Peace be with you. Do not be afraid. The Lord has blessed you. God is asking you to be the mother of His Son.

Mary: How can this be?

Gabriel: The Holy Spirit will come to you. God can do anything.

Mary: I am the Lord's servant. I will do as He asks.

Narrator: Mary has a cousin named Elizabeth. Elizabeth is expecting a baby. Mary goes to visit her. When Elizabeth sees Mary, Elizabeth is filled with joy from God.

Elizabeth: Mary, you are the most blessed of all women and blessed is the child you will have.

Mary: My heart praises the Lord. God has kept His promise and has come to help us.

Lesson 23: Christmas

Narrator: Mary visits with Elizabeth. After several months Mary goes back home.

Act 2

Narrator: After Joseph and Mary are married a ruler named Caesar Augustus wants to know how many people he rules.

Caesar: I want to know how many people I rule.

Soldier: How will you do this?

Caesar: I will have all the people go back to their home towns. There they will be registered and counted.

Narrator: Joseph's family was from Bethelehem, so this is where Mary and Joseph go. It is a long journey from Nazareth. Joseph is worried about Mary because it is almost time for her to have her baby.

Joseph: Mary, I know the journey to Bethlehem is long. I have bought a donkey so that you can ride.

Mary: Don't worry about me, Joseph. I will be fine.

Narrator: Mary and Joseph pack their bags on the donkey. They begin the long journey to Bethlehem. When they finally arrive in Bethlehem, the city is very crowded. Many people have come to register. Mary and Joseph try hard to find a place to stay.

(Joseph knocks on the first inn's door.)

Amos: Who's there?

Joseph: It is two travelers. We are looking for a room for the night.

Lesson 23: Christmas

Amos: Sorry, I am completely full. You will have to try someplace else.

Narrator: Joseph and Mary walk to another inn.

(Joseph knocks on the door.)

Zach:
(grumpily) What do you want?

Joseph: We need a place to stay.

Zach: Forget it! I am already full. (He slams the door.)

Narrator: Joseph and Mary walk towards the end of town, hoping to find someone who has a room for them.

(Joseph knocks on the third inn's door.)

Michael: How may I help you?

Joseph: My wife and I need a place to stay.

Michael: Bethlehem is so crowded! I don't have any rooms left.

Joseph: Please, isn't there some place you could let us stay? My wife is about to have a baby.

Michael: Well . . . the only place I can offer is the stable. The animals are there, but at least you would be out of the wind.

Joseph: Thank you, we will stay there.

Mary: Joseph, let's hurry. I think the baby will be born soon.

Lesson 23: Christmas

Narrator:	Mary and Joseph walk to the stable. During the night, Mary has her baby.
Mary:	He is a beautiful baby. We shall call Him Jesus. Let's wrap Him in swaddling clothes. We will use the manger as a crib.

Act 3

Narrator:	Nearby, there are shepherds in the fields, watching their sheep. Suddenly, the sky is filled with a bright light and the shepherds are afraid. The shepherds look up and see many angels in the sky.
Angel:	Do not be afraid. I have come to tell you good news. Today, in the city of Bethlehem, a Savior has been born to you. You will find Him in a manger, wrapped in swaddling clothes.
Narrator:	The angels begin to praise God.
Angels:	Glory to God in the highest, peace to His people on earth.
Narrator:	The angels then return to heaven. The shepherds began to talk and to decide what to do.
Seth:	Let's go visit this baby.
Tim:	We are lucky the angels have told us about this baby.
Narrator:	The shepherds hurry off to find Baby Jesus. They find Mary and Joseph in the stable. Jesus is there, lying in the manger, wrapped in swaddling clothes.
Mary:	Thank you for visiting us. I will always remember what you have told us.

Lesson 23: Christmas

Narrator: Before the shepherds leave, they praise God.

Seth: God, thank you for sending us a Savior.

Andrew: You are wonderful, God. Thank you for letting us see the Savior.

Narrator: The shepherds leave. They tell everyone what they have seen and what they have been told.

Act 4

Narrator: Sometime after Jesus was born, three wise men arrive in Jerusalem. Their names are Melchior, Gaspar, and Balthasar. They have been following a bright star. They go to King Herod for help.

Melchior: Where is the newborn King of the Jews?

Gaspar: We saw His star rising and have come to praise Him.

Narrator: King Herod is upset. He talks to his advisors.

King Herod: Who is this King the wise men are talking about?

Advisors: A prophet has written that in Bethlehem a King will come who will be a leader of the Israelite people.

Narrator: King Herod is afraid that this King will take over his kingdom. He wants to find Him before this can happen. King Herod talks to the wise men.

King Herod: This child is in Bethlehem. Go and find Him. Get all the information you can. Then come back and tell me about this child so I can honor Him, too.

The three wise men follow the star again. They follow the star until it stops. It shines above the place where Jesus is. The wise men go inside and see Mary and Jesus. They bow to Jesus and praise Him. The wise men give Jesus gifts.

Balthasar: Here is a gift of frankincense.

Gaspar: I have brought you a gift of gold.

Melchior: This is a gift of myrrh.

Mary: Thank you very much.

Narrator: During the night, the wise men receive a message in a dream.

Angel: Do not return to King Herod. He is afraid that Jesus will take over his kingdom. He wants to hurt Jesus. Do not go back and talk to King Herod.

Narrator: The wise men believe the angel and go back to their own country without stopping to see King Herod.

After the wise men leave, an angel appears to Joseph in a dream.

Angel: Wake up, Joseph. Get up and take Jesus and Mary to Egypt. Stay there until it is safe to come back. King Herod is looking for Jesus. He wants to hurt Him.

Narrator: Joseph wakes up. He believes the angel and gets His family ready to leave.

Joseph: Mary, get Jesus. We must leave quickly. An angel has told me it is not safe to stay here.

Narrator: So Jesus, Mary, and Joseph leave Bethlehem that night for Egypt.

STATIONS OF THE CROSS

Lesson 24: Lent

SECOND STATION

Jesus Takes His Cross

Leader: Jesus must have been tired after the soldiers beat Him and made Him wear a crown of thorns. Then the soldiers gave Him the heavy wooden cross to carry all the way to the hill outside the city.

Children: Jesus, You did not complain when You received Your cross. I sometimes have to do things that I do not like to do. When this happens, I will try to be more like You. I will pretend it is my cross to carry and I will carry it without complaining.

2.

FIRST STATION

Jesus is Condemned to Death

Leader: The soldiers have arrested Jesus. They put a crown of thorns on Jesus and make fun of Him. Then Pilate gives an order to have Jesus put to death. Jesus did not fight back. He knew this was what God the Father wished Him to do. His Father asked Him to die on the cross as a sacrifice of love.

Directions: Color the picture below.

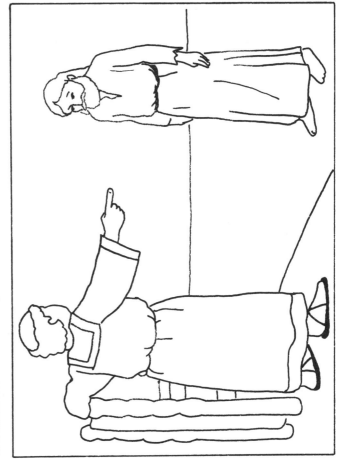

Children: Jesus, I know I need to always obey my parents. This is not always easy for me to do. When I am tempted to disobey, I will remember how obedient You are. Jesus, I will try to act more like You.

1.

FOURTH STATION

Jesus Meets His Mother

Leader: Jesus is carrying the heavy cross. The soldiers are walking beside Him. Jesus looks up and sees His Mother. He knows how much Mary loves Him. It must be hard for Mary to see Jesus suffering. She loves Him so much.

Children: Jesus, I have people who love me and care for me. When I am having a bad day, I am glad there is someone who loves me and can help me feel better. You also gave me Your Mother, Mary, to love and to care for me. Thank You, Jesus.

4.

THIRD STATION

Jesus Falls the First Time

Leader: Jesus is tired from His beatings. As Jesus walks, the cross becomes heavier. Jesus falls down. Jesus knows He must continue, so He gets back up. Jesus picks up the cross and continues His journey.

Directions: Color the picture below.

Children: Jesus, sometimes I get tired and it is hard to finish my work. When I am tempted to quit before I complete my work, I am going to think about You. Jesus, please help me to do my best and to finish my jobs.

3.

145

SIXTH STATION

Veronica Wipes Jesus' Face

Leader: Veronica sees that Jesus is hot and tired. She wonders what she can do to help him. Veronica finds a cloth. She wipes the sweat and blood off Jesus' face.

Children: Jesus, help me be like Veronica. Please help me to notice people who need help and I will try to help them.

6.

FIFTH STATION

Jesus is Helped by Simon

Leader: Jesus is very tired. The soldiers decide Jesus needs help. The solders pull Simon from the crowd. They make him help Jesus carry the cross.

Directions: Color the picture below.

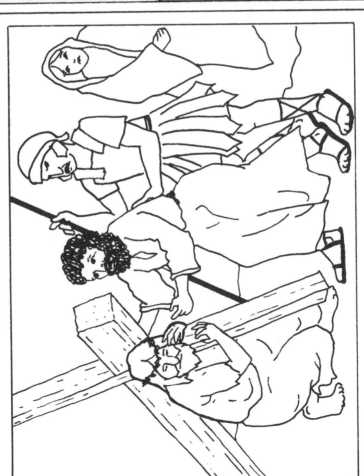

Children: Jesus, sometimes I need help but I do not want to admit it. Instead, I get angry and upset. Please help me be patient and accept people's help

5.

147

EIGHTH STATION

Jesus Meets the Women

Leader: Jesus continues His long, hard walk. He looks up and sees several women who are friends of His. They do not understand why Jesus is going to die. They are very sad and are crying.

Children: Jesus, sometimes I am like the women. I do not understand why some things happen. I pray to You and I do not receive the answer that I thought I would. Please help me have faith to believe that You will do what is best for me.

SEVENTH STATION

Jesus Falls a Second Time

Leader: Even with Simon's help, Jesus stumbles and falls. Jesus knows His journey is not over yet. Somehow, Jesus stands back up and continues to walk.

Directions: Color the picture below.

Children: Jesus, sometimes I make mistakes. I cannot seem to do anything right. I become afraid to try to do anything. You must have felt that it was impossible to keep walking, but You did! Jesus, please give me courage to keep on trying, even if it seems impossible.

TENTH STATION

Jesus is Stripped of His Clothes

Leader: Jesus arrives at the hill outside Jerusalem. The soldiers take off Jesus' clothes. The people will make fun of Him for not saving Himself. Jesus knows His Father still loves Him a lot.

Directions: Color the picture below.

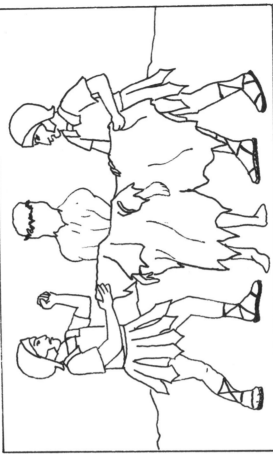

Children: If my clothes were taken from me, I would be really hurt and upset. Jesus, You never said a word and You did not fight back. Sometimes, I do what I know is right but everyone makes fun of me. Then I get embarrassed. Next time this happens, I will think about You, Jesus—and I will not change my choice and I will not say anything mean back to the people who are teasing me.

10.

NINTH STATION

Jesus Falls a Third Time

Leader: Jesus stumbles and falls again. This time it takes longer for Him to stand up again. It has been a long walk but it is almost over.

Children: Jesus, You have fallen again, but You get back up. Sometimes I fall by making the same wrong choice, again and again. I know You want me to be sorry for my wrong choice. You want me to get up, to keep going, and to try to do better. Thank You, Jesus, for forgiving me and helping me make the right choices.

9.

TWELFTH STATION

Jesus Dies

Leader: Jesus dies. A soldier puts his sword in Jesus' side to make sure Jesus is dead. Jesus performs the greatest sacrifice of love, He dies on the cross for us.

Children: Jesus, You love us so much that You died on the cross for us. I cannot imagine how much it must have hurt to have Your hands and feet nailed to a cross. I know You do not expect me to die on the cross to show my love for You. However, I will try to do small sacrifices to show my love for You, Jesus.

12.

ELEVENTH STATION

Jesus is Nailed to the Cross

Leader: The soldiers nail Jesus to the cross. Nails are pounded into His hands and feet. The soldiers lift up the cross and put it in place.

Directions: Color the picture below.

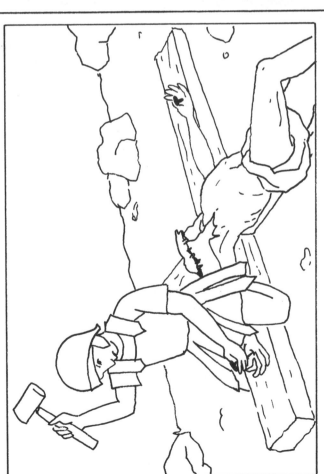

Children: Jesus, I cannot imagine how much pain You must have felt. This was a real sacrifice of love. As a sign of my love for You, I am going to try to do sacrifices. I will give up my favorite T.V. program, or I will give up chocolate, or I will do something else that is hard for me to do.

11.

FOURTEENTH STATION

Jesus is Buried in a Tomb

Leader: Jesus is wrapped in fresh linen with perfumed oils. He is laid in a new tomb that has never been used. In just three days He will rise from the dead.

Directions: Color the picture below.

Children: Jesus, You did everything God the Father asked You to do. Please help me be more like You. Help me to remember to act as an image of God. Thank You, Jesus, for loving me.

14.

THIRTEENTH STATION

Jesus is Taken Down From The Cross

Leader: Jesus is taken down from the cross. He is laid in His Mother's arms. Mary must feel a lot of sorrow as she holds Jesus' lifeless body.

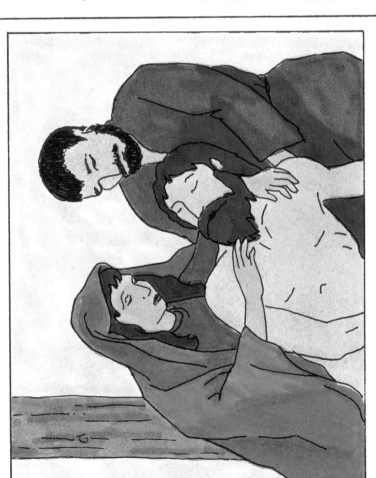

Children: Mary must have felt really sad as she held Jesus' body. I know there are people around me who are sad and lonely. Jesus, help me to notice these people and to do something to help them feel better.

13.

155

Lesson 25: Easter

The women saw Jesus after He had risen. They hugged Jesus and praised Him. Write a prayer praising Jesus for everything He has done.

_____

_____

_____

_____

_____

_____

Lesson 25: Easter

On Easter Sunday evening, after Jesus had risen from the dead, ten of the Apostles were gathered in a large room together. The doors were locked because they were afraid of the people who had hurt Jesus. Suddenly Jesus stood before them. Jesus said, "Peace be with you." Then Jesus showed the Apostles the wounds in His hands, His feet, and His side. The Apostles were so happy to see Jesus alive!

One of the Apostles named Thomas was not in the room that night when Jesus came. The other Apostles kept telling him, "We have seen the Lord!" Poor Thomas had a hard time believing what they were saying. He said that he wanted to see and to touch Jesus' wounds.

A week later, the Apostles were gathered in the room again, and this time Thomas was with them. Even though the doors were locked, Jesus stood before them. Jesus showed Thomas the wounds in His hands, His feet, and His side. Then Thomas believed that Jesus had risen. Thomas said, "My Lord and my God!"

We receive faith when we are baptized.
Through faith we believe that
Jesus is risen.

We also believe that He is
with us through the Church.

Lesson 26: The Rosary

Directions: Match the name of each mystery with the correct picture by drawing a line from the name of the mystery to the picture of the same mystery.

THE JOYFUL MYSTERIES

1. Annunciation
2. Visitation
3. Nativity
4. Presentation
5. Finding in the Temple

Directions: *Match the name of each mystery with the correct picture by drawing a line from the name of the mystery to the picture of the same mystery.*

THE SORROWFUL MYSTERIES

1. Agony in the Garden

2. Scourging at the Pillar

3. Crowning with Thorns

4. Carrying of the Cross

5. Crucifixion

Directions: Match the name of each mystery with the correct picture by drawing a line from the name of the mystery to the picture of the same mystery.

THE GLORIOUS MYSTERIES

1. The Resurrection
2. Ascension
3. Descent of the Holy Spirit
4. Assumption
5. Coronation

Lesson 26: The Rosary

Directions: Next to the crucifix; the medal; each bead, or set of beads; and certain spaces; there are lines. On the lines next to the crucifix, medal, bead or set of beads, and spaces, write the appropriate prayer that is said in that spot.

APOSTLES' CREED

I believe in God, the Father almighty,
creator of heaven and earth.

I believe in Jesus Christ, his only Son, our Lord.
He was conceived by the power of the Holy Spirit
and born of the Virgin Mary.
He suffered under Pontius Pilate,
was crucified, died, and was buried.
He descended to the dead.
On the third day he rose again.
He ascended into heaven,
and is seated at the right hand of the Father.
He will come again to judge the living and the dead.

I believe in the Holy Spirit,
the holy catholic Church,
the communion of saints,
the forgiveness of sins,
the resurrection of the body,
and the life everlasting. Amen.

HAIL HOLY QUEEN

Hail, holy Queen, Mother of Mercy, our life,
our sweetness, and our hope! To thee do we
cry, poor banished children of Eve;
to thee do we send up our sighs, mourning and
weeping in this valley of tears. Turn, then, most
gracious advocate, thine eyes of mercy toward us,
and after this our exile show unto us the blessed
fruit of thy womb, Jesus. O clement, O loving,
O sweet Virgin Mary.

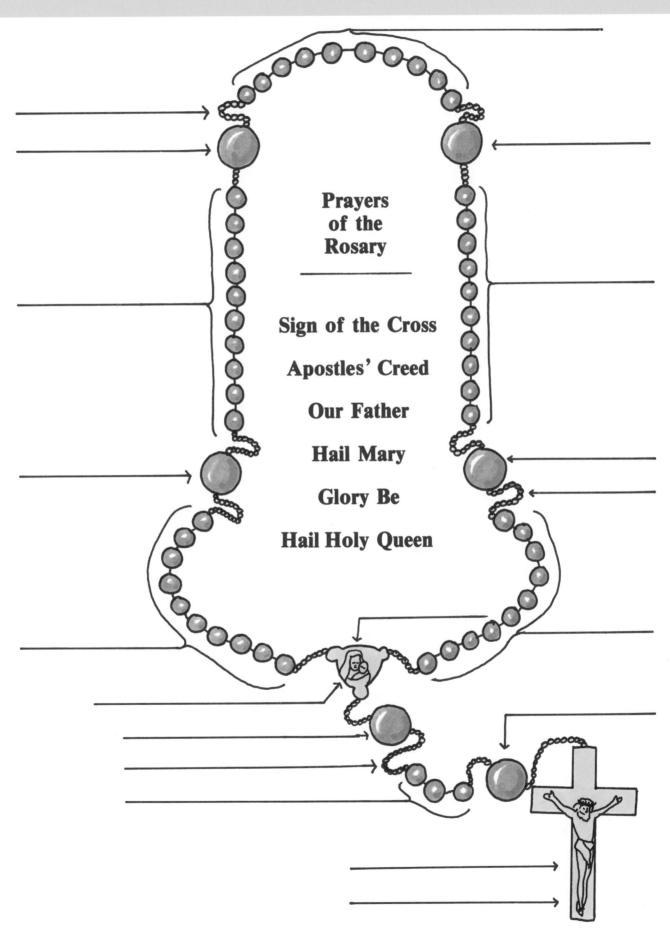

Prayers
of the
Rosary

Sign of the Cross

Apostles' Creed

Our Father

Hail Mary

Glory Be

Hail Holy Queen

Lesson 26: The Rosary

Directions: Cut out the holy card below and use it as a bookmark or give it as a gift to someone.

"To Our Lady"

Lovely Lady dressed in blue—
Teach me how to pray!
God was just your little Boy,
Tell me what to say!

Did you lift Him up, sometimes,
Gently, on your knee?
Did you sing to Him, the way
Mother does to me?

Do you really think He cares
If I tell Him things—
Little things that happen? And
Do the Angels' wings

Make a noise? And can He hear
Me if I speak low?
Does He understand me now?
Tell me—for you know.

Lovely Lady dressed in blue,
Teach me how to pray!
God was just your little Boy,
And you know the way.

Lesson 27: Holy Days

Directions: Fill in the blanks with the name of the Holy Day that fits each statement.

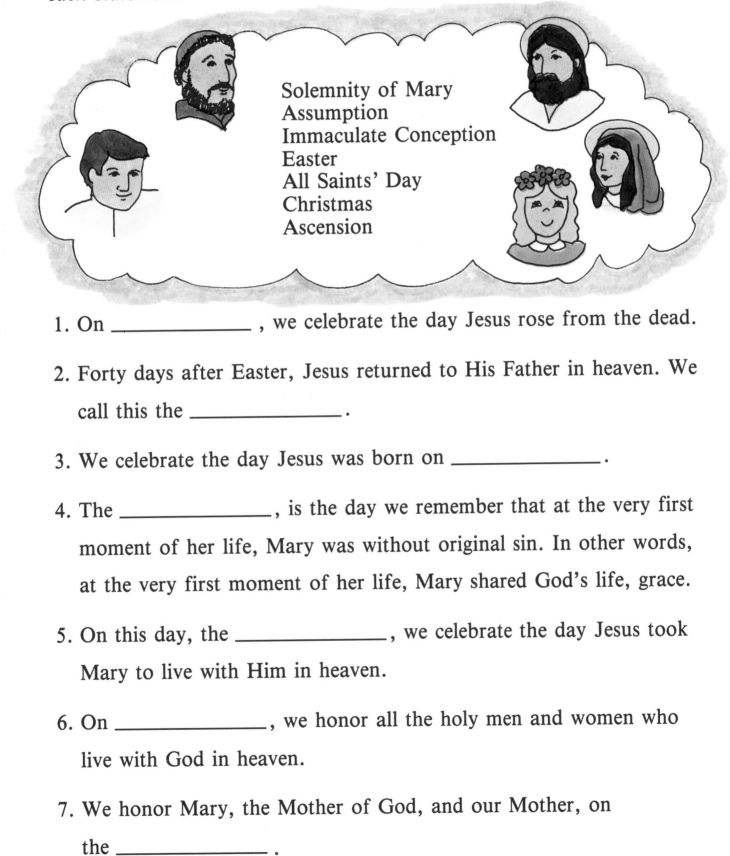

Solemnity of Mary
Assumption
Immaculate Conception
Easter
All Saints' Day
Christmas
Ascension

1. On _____ , we celebrate the day Jesus rose from the dead.

2. Forty days after Easter, Jesus returned to His Father in heaven. We call this the _____.

3. We celebrate the day Jesus was born on _____.

4. The _____, is the day we remember that at the very first moment of her life, Mary was without original sin. In other words, at the very first moment of her life, Mary shared God's life, grace.

5. On this day, the _____, we celebrate the day Jesus took Mary to live with Him in heaven.

6. On _____, we honor all the holy men and women who live with God in heaven.

7. We honor Mary, the Mother of God, and our Mother, on the _____.

Our Father

Our Father, Who art in heaven,
hallowed be Thy name;
Thy kingdom come;
Thy will be done on earth as it is in heaven.
Give us this day our daily bread;
and forgive us our trespasses as we forgive those who trespass against us;
and lead us not into temptation, but deliver us from evil.
Amen.

Apostles' Creed

I believe in God, the Father almighty,
    Creator of heaven and earth.
I believe in Jesus Christ, His only Son, our Lord.
    He was conceived by the power of the Holy Spirit
        and born of the Virgin Mary.
    He suffered under Pontius Pilate,
        was crucified, died, and was buried.
    He descended to the dead.
    On the third day He rose again.
    He ascended into heaven,
        and is seated at the right hand of the Father.
    He will come again to judge the living and the dead.
I believe in the Holy Spirit,
    the holy Catholic Church,
    the communion of saints,
    the forgiveness of sins,
    the resurrection of the body,
    and the life everlasting.
Amen.

Glory Be

Glory be to the Father, and to the Son, and to the Holy Spirit,
as it was in the beginning, is now, and ever shall be, world without end.
Amen.

Hail Mary

Hail, Mary, full of grace, the Lord is with thee.
Blessed art thou among women, and blessed is the fruit of thy womb, Jesus.
Holy Mary, Mother of God, pray for us sinners now and at the hour of our death.
Amen.

Hail, Holy Queen

Hail, holy Queen, Mother of mercy,
     our life, our sweetness and our hope.
To you do we cry, poor banished children of Eve.
To you do we send up our sighs,
     mourning and weeping in this vale of tears.
Turn then, most gracious advocate,
     your eyes of mercy toward us,
     and after this exile
     show to us the blessed fruit of your womb, Jesus.
O clement, O loving, O sweet Virgin Mary.
     V. Pray for us, O holy Mother of God.
     R. That we may be made worthy of the promises of Christ.

Angelus

The angel of the Lord declared unto Mary:
And she conceived by the Holy Spirit.
     Hail, Mary, . . .
Behold the handmaid of the Lord:
Be it done to me according to Your word.
     Hail, Mary, . . .
And the Word was made flesh:
And dwelt among us.
     Hail, Mary, . . .
Pray for us, O holy Mother of God:
That we may be made worthy of the promises of Christ.
     Pour forth, we beseech You, O Lord, Your grace into our hearts, that we to
     whom the Incarnation of Christ, Your Son, was made known by the message
     of an angel, may by His Passion and Cross be brought to the glory of His
     resurrection. Through Christ our Lord. Amen.

Memorare

Remember, O most gracious Virgin Mary,
    that never was it known
    that anyone who fled to your protection,
    implored your help,
    or sought your intercession,
    was left unaided.
Inspired by this confidence,
    I fly unto you, O Virgin of virgins, my Mother.
To you do I come, before you I stand, sinful and sorrowful.
O Mother of the Word Incarnate,
    despise not my petitions,
    but in your mercy hear and answer me.
Amen.

Act of Contrition

My God,
I am sorry for my sins with all my heart.
In choosing to do wrong and failing to do good,
I have sinned against You,
    Whom I should love above all things.
I have hurt myself and others.
I firmly intend, with Your help,
    to do penance, to sin no more,
    and to avoid whatever leads me to sin.
Our Savior Jesus Christ suffered and died for us.
In His name, my God, have mercy.
Amen.

An Act of Faith

O my God, I firmly believe that You are one God in three Divine Persons,
    Father, Son, and Holy Spirit.
I believe that Your Divine Son became man and died for our sins,
    and that He will come to judge the living and the dead.
I believe these and all the truths which the holy Catholic Church teaches,
    because You have revealed them, Who can neither deceive nor be deceived.
Amen.

Morning Offering

O Jesus, through the Immaculate Heart of Mary,
I offer You my prayers, works, joys, and sufferings of this day
in union with the Holy Sacrifice of the Mass throughout the world.
I offer them for all the intentions of Your Sacred Heart:
the salvation of souls,
reparation for sin,
the reunion of all Christians.
I offer them for the intentions of our bishops and of all Apostles of Prayer,
and in particular for those recommended by our Holy Father this month.
Amen.

—Apostleship of Prayer

Grace before Meals

Bless us, O Lord, and these Thy gifts,
which we are about to receive from Thy bounty.
Through Christ our Lord. Amen.

Grace after Meals

We give Thee thanks for all Thy gifts, almighty God.
You live and reign forever.
Amen.

An Act of Hope

O my God, relying on Your infinite goodness and promises,
    I hope to obtain pardon of my sins,
    the help of Your grace,
    and life everlasting,
    through the merits of Jesus Christ, my Lord and Redeemer.
Amen.

An Act of Love

O my God, I love You above all things,
    with my whole heart and soul,
    because You are all-good and worthy of all my love.
I love my neighbor as myself for the love of You.
I forgive all who have injured me,
    and ask pardon of all whom I have injured.
Amen.

NOTES

NOTES

NOTES

NOTES